HOW TO PRACTICE

MINDFULNESS

FOR DAILY LIFE

Reduce Stress, Focus Your Mind, Improves Physical and Mental Health, The Difference It Can Make

MICHAEL GOODRICH

TABLE OF CONTENT

- 6 Simple Tips to Practice Mindfulness Every Day

- How Mindfulness Helps Us Be More Present

- 21 simple mindfulness exercises to improve your focus

Mindfulness exercises

Common Mindfulness Questions

What is mindfulness?

The official definition: Mindfulness is paying attention, on purpose, in the present moment, without judgment.

What that really means: Mindfulness is a state of being when your body and mind are in the same place at the same time. That means bringing attention to what you are doing and where you are, without worrying about the future or the past.

Think of it like you're sitting at your desk and eating a granola bar and all of a sudden you're aware that you're sitting at your desk and eating a granola bar. You're not worried about what you're going to eat for dinner or thinking about how you embarrassed yourself earlier this morning. You're just in that moment, as it happens.

What that looks like in daily life: Most of us spend our days half-aware of what we're doing and what we're thinking. We live on autopilot and go through our routines without noticing what we're doing unless our routine is thrown off.

Mindfulness develops by noticing mindlessness and using this awareness to be more intentional with your actions. If you can bring more intention to your routines and take time to schedule in mindfulness practices, you can begin to reap the benefits of mindfulness.

What Mindfulness Is Not

Despite its roots in Eastern religion, mindfulness isn't inherently religious. Mindfulness is a secular practice that can be used by those who practice religion and those who don't. As someone who is not religious, I find mindfulness has actually allowed me to connect with my spiritual side.

Mindfulness is also not synonymous with meditation. Rather, meditation is a practice that helps us to be more mindful (we'll talk about types of mindfulness practices later).

The History and Origin of Mindfulness

One of the (numerous) reasons Jon Kabat-Zinn is so widely linked to the concept of mindfulness is because he is generally accepted as having "re-imagined Buddhist contemplation practices for a secular age almost 40 years ago". From this sentence alone, we already know two things.

First, mindfulness practices have been around for a very long time. Second, we can trace at least a large amount of its current popularity in the Western world to Dr. Kabat-Zinn's work on MBSR (Shea, 2018). We've actually covered a lot of the ancient roots of mindfulness elsewhere in our article on The History of Mindfulness, so for now, we'll take a peek at its growth in more recent decades.

Kabat-Zinn's own story is inspiring, to say the least, and a good place to start. As an MIT student, he became acquainted with Buddhist philosophies when he met Philip Kapleau, a Zen practitioner who gave a speech at the Institute. He then went on to develop MBSR within a scientific setting, bringing his learning from many years of meditation teaching to the field. In 1979, he established the University of Massachusetts Medical Clinic's Stress Reduction School, where MBSR really came to the fore.

As the concept gained more traction, Kabat-Zinn published a popular book called Full Living Catastrophe, which also played a significant role in making mindfulness practice and meditation much more accessible to mainstream circles. Inspired by the myriad secular applications of mindfulness, practitioners across the world have now adopted the practice within both specialized settings and everyday contexts.

So what exactly have we taken from Buddhism? Let's have a look.

What Is the Meaning of Mindfulness?

It's not uncommon for people to equate mindfulness with meditation. It's true that meditation is one extremely powerful way to practice mindfulness, but that's not all there is to it.

According to the American Psychological Association mindfulness is:

> "…a moment-to-moment awareness of one's experience without judgment. In this sense, mindfulness is a state and not a trait. While it might be promoted by certain practices or activities, such as meditation, it is not equivalent to or synonymous with them."

As we can see, mindfulness is a state that can be brought on through practice. It's not static, nor are some people 'born more mindful' than others. It involves awareness, and impartiality about what we gain from this awareness. In an age of social media, where opinions, likes, and commentary are more than forthcoming, it's easy to see how non-judgmental reflection can be a welcome change.

Another definition comes from Jon Kabat Zinn, who enjoys significant global renown for his work on mindfulness-based stress reduction:

> "The awareness that arises from paying attention, on purpose, in the present moment and non- judgmentally"

This is the more widely accepted definition in practitioner and academic literature, and perhaps more descriptive for those who want to start practicing. As well as awareness, Kabat-Zinn tells us to focus conscious attention on the 'right here, right now'. It's a concept that most who practice meditation will already be familiar with, and it's why the two often go hand in hand.

The Importance of Mindfulness

Whether you want to practice mindfulness to deal with anxiety or stress, or whether you're keen to improve your attentional skills, there's plenty of scientific evidence in your favor.

Mindfulness can help us cope with depression, boost our psychological well-being, manage physical pain, and even have better memory. When it comes to the way we think and feel, being mindful of our emotions helps us to switch to more positive mindsets and work towards being a 'better'—or at least, a happier— person.

In terms of relationships, as we'll see in a short while, it has positive implications for how we communicate and relate to those around us.

Nonetheless, all the studies have one thing in common. That is, to reap the benefits, you'll want to find a method of mindfulness practice that works for you.

Through practice, whether it be an intervention or meditation, we can learn to cultivate the state of mind that lets us be mindful when we feel we need it most. If you choose to take an online course, or download scripts to help you on-the-go, you're already well on the way to your goal.

Don't worry. A bit further on, we'll get a little bit more specific, giving some examples of just how mindfulness can play an important helping role in your daily life.

Why is mindfulness so popular?

Mindfulness has been around for thousands of years with roots in Eastern religions such as Hinduism and Buddhism. However, mindfulness became increasingly popular in the West primarily because of Jon Kabat-Zinn who created the Mindfulness-Based Stress Reduction program in the 1970s.

In the early 2000s, there was an explosion of research in mindfulness interventions which could explain why mindfulness has become so popular today. In a society where busyness and burnout are the norm, mindfulness offers an alternate experience of living that has been shown to provide enormous benefits.

Why practice mindfulness?

Mindfulness helps us to connect with ourselves and others, react productively to stressful situations, and find more balance in our busy lives. Research on mindfulness has shown that there are many benefits* to mindfulness, including:

Decreased stress response

Increased immune system activity

Increased capacity for compassion

Improved ability to regulate emotions

Increased ability to relax

Improvements in chronic pain levels

Improvements in anxiety and depression symptoms

Improved ability to experience moments with greater clarity and objectivity

Personally, I've noticed that mindfulness helps me reduce anxious thoughts, think more clearly, and actually enjoy the little moments in life.

*It's important to note that much of the research on mindfulness is done in controlled groups led by trained professionals, so the results might not always be the same if you are simply practicing mindfulness without guidance.

To truly make mindfulness part of you life, you need to have the right attitude and mindset.

1. Non-Judging: Noticing when you're being judgmental of yourself and others

Patience: Letting things unfold in their own time without rushing

3. Beginner's Mind: Being receptive to new possibilities and realizing you don't need to know all of the answers

4. Trust: Trusting in yourself and taking responsibility for your actions

5. Non-Striving: Not forcing certain results to happen and letting things happen in their own time

6. Acceptance: Accepting things as they are in the moment without denying or trying to change things

7. Letting Go: Being willing to let go of the things, people, or ideas that prevent you from living in the moment

Types of Mindfulness

In order to make mindfulness part of your life, you need to make it a regular practice. Mindfulness practices are essential because they encourage us to focus on the present moment even during busy and stressful times. Taking five minutes out of your day to practice mindfulness can make a difference. Here are some different types of mindfulness practices (although the list goes on and on):

Yin Yoga: A slow-paced type of yoga where poses are held for long period of times

Qigong: A form of gentle exercise that focuses on repetition and slow movement

Mindful Eating: Practicing the art of eating slowly without distraction

Body Scan Meditation: Scanning the body to bring awareness to bodily sensations

Loving-Kindness Meditation: a form of meditation that focuses on sending kindness and compassion towards others and self

Benefits of Mindfulness

What are the benefits of mindfulness?

The cultivation of mindfulness has roots in Buddhism, but most religions include some type of prayer or meditation technique that helps shift your thoughts away from your usual preoccupations toward an appreciation of the moment and a larger perspective on life.

Professor emeritus Jon Kabat-Zinn, founder and former director of the Stress Reduction Clinic at the University of Massachusetts Medical Center, helped to bring the practice of mindfulness meditation into mainstream medicine and demonstrated that practicing mindfulness can bring improvements in both physical and psychological symptoms as well as positive changes in health, attitudes, and behaviors.

Mindfulness improves well-being. Increasing your capacity for mindfulness supports many attitudes that contribute to a satisfied life. Being mindful makes it easier to savor the pleasures in life as they occur, helps you become fully engaged in activities, and creates a greater capacity to deal with adverse events. By focusing on the here and now, many people who practice mindfulness find that they are less likely to get caught up in worries about the future or regrets over the past, are less preoccupied with concerns about success and self-esteem, and are better able to form deep connections with others.

Mindfulness improves physical health. If greater well-being isn't enough of an incentive, scientists have discovered that mindfulness techniques help improve physical health in a number of ways. Mindfulness can:

help relieve stress, treat heart disease, lower blood pressure, reduce chronic pain, , improve sleep, and alleviate gastrointestinal difficulties.

Mindfulness improves mental health. In recent years, psychotherapists have turned to mindfulness meditation as an important element in the treatment of a number of problems, including: depression, substance abuse, eating disorders, couples' conflicts, anxiety disorders, and obsessive-compulsive disorder.

How does mindfulness work?

Some experts believe that mindfulness works, in part, by helping people to accept their experiences - including painful emotions—rather than react to them with aversion and avoidance.

It's become increasingly common for mindfulness meditation to be combined with psychotherapy, especially cognitive behavioral therapy. This development makes good sense, since both meditation and cognitive behavioral therapy share the common goal of helping people gain perspective on irrational, maladaptive, and self- defeating thoughts.

7 Benefits According to the Research

Mindfulness practice has been associated with numerous benefits, and the popularity of the topic in positive psychology means that we'll probably be seeing a lot more to come. Take a look at this graph, for instance

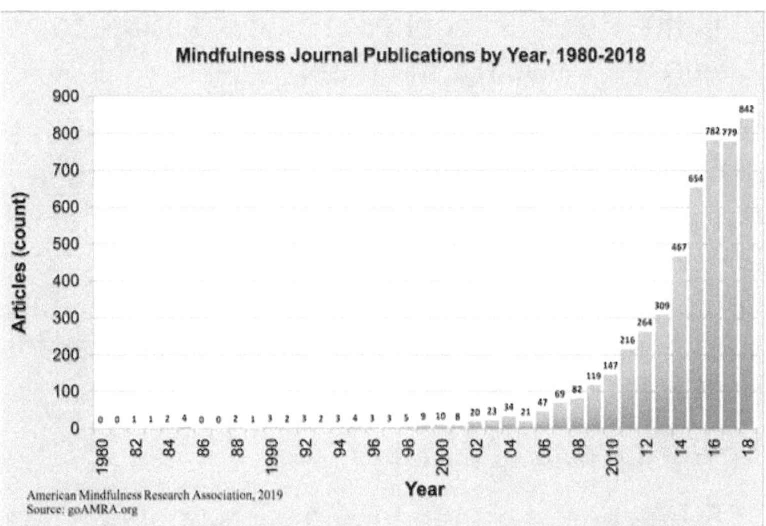

The following are just a few examples of what the literature has shown.

1. Improved Working Memory

According to a study by Jha and colleagues in 2010, mindfulness meditation has been empirically linked to enhanced working memory capacity. Comparing samples of military participants who practiced mindfulness meditation training for eight weeks with those who didn't, Jha et al. (2010) found evidence to suggest that mindfulness training helped 'buffer' against losses to working memory capacity.

They also found that working memory capacity also increased as the first group practiced mindfulness meditation. These participants also reported greater positive affect and lowered negative affect.

2. Heightened Metacognitive Awareness

In layperson's terms, this describes being able to detach from one's own feelings and mental processes—to step back and perceive them as transient, momentary occurrences rather than 'who we are'. In the Buddhist sense, this would relate to 'knowing' and 'freeing' the mind.

With regard to the empirical literature, it describes how mindfulness has been hypothesized to decrease patterns of negative thinking behavior (Teasdale, 1999), increased metacognitive awareness, and decentering (Fresco et al., 2007). In turn, this may have a positive effect in helping avoid relapses into depression (Teasdale, 1999).

3. Lower Levels of Anxiety

MBSR has been examined in a wide host of randomized, controlled trials that find support for its impact on alleviating symptoms of anxiety. Vøllestad and colleagues, for instance, found that participants who completed MBSR had a medium to large positive impact on anxiety symptoms (Vøllestad et al., 2011).

Similar results have also been found in studies on social anxiety disorder (SAD). For example, that of Goldin and Gross (2010), who found evidence to suggest MBSR training in SAD patients helped to improve in anxiety and depression symptoms, as well as self-esteem.

4. Reduced Emotional 'Reactivity'

There is also evidence to support the role of mindfulness meditation in emotive 'reactivity'. In an emotional interference task conducted by Ortner and colleagues in 2007, participants with wide-ranging experience in mindfulness meditation were asked to categorize tones that were given either 1 or 4 seconds after a neutral or emotionally upsetting picture was presented.

Those with more experience practicing mindfulness meditation were better able to disengage emotionally, meaning that they showed greater focus on the task at hand even when emotionally upsetting pictures were shown (Ortner et al., 2007).

5. Enhanced Visual Attention Processing

Another study by Hodgins and Adair (2010) compared the performance of 'meditators' and 'non-meditators' on visual attention processing tasks. Those who practiced mindfulness meditation showed greater attentional functioning through better performance on tests of concentration, selective attention, and more.

These results correspond with earlier findings that systematic mindfulness meditation training stimulates improvements in attention, awareness, and emotion

6. Reduced Stress

Mindfulness training has also been linked to loer stress levels. One example of empirical evidence comes from Bränström et al. (2010), who found cancer patients who took part in mindfulness training had significanly reduced self-reported stress than those who didn't. They also displayed greater positive states of mind and fewer post-traumatic avoidance symptoms, such as loss of interest in activities.

7. Managing Physical Pain

There is also research that suggests mindfulness may have a role in helping to manage subjective pain. Those interested in further reading may like Kieszkowska-Grudny's (2016) review of the literature on this topic. In it, she includes numerous examples of studies into how mindfulness may help to manage chronic pain and help patients improve their quality of life (e.g. Goldenberg et al., 1994; Vowles &

McCracken, 2008; 2011).

This list is by no means exhaustive. Indeed, there are lots more studies into topics such as reduced psychological distress, heightened focus, and plenty more applications of the above ideas in much more specific settings. But hopefully, this is enough to begin looking at how mindfulness can help us in our daily lives.

Mindfulness techniques

There is more than one way to practice mindfulness, but the goal of any mindfulness technique is to achieve a state of alert, focused relaxation by deliberately paying attention to thoughts and sensations without judgment. This allows the mind to refocus on the present moment. All mindfulness techniques are a form of meditation.

Basic mindfulness meditation – Sit quietly and focus on your natural breathing or on a word or "mantra" that you repeat silently. Allow thoughts to come and go without judgment and return to your focus on breath or mantra.

Body sensations – Notice subtle body sensations such as an itch or tingling without judgment and let them pass. Notice each part of your body in succession from head to toe.

Sensory – Notice sights, sounds, smells, tastes, and touches. Name them "sight," "sound," "smell," "taste," or "touch" without judgment and let them go.

Emotions – Allow emotions to be present without judgment. Practice a steady and relaxed naming of emotions: "joy," "anger," "frustration." Accept the presence of the emotions without judgment and let them go.

Urge surfing – Cope with cravings (for addictive substances or behaviors) and allow them to pass. Notice how your body feels as the craving enters. Replace the wish for the craving to go away with the certain knowledge that it will subside.

8 Facts About Mindfulness:

1. Mindfulness is not obscure or exotic. It's familiar to us because it's what we already do, how we already are. It takes many shapes and goes by many names.

2. Mindfulness is not a special added thing we do. We already have the capacity to be present, and it doesn't require us to change who we are. But we can cultivate these innate qualities with simple practices that are scientifically demonstrated to benefit ourselves, our loved ones, our friends and neighbors, the people we work with, and the institutions and organizations we take part in

3. You don't need to change. Solutions that ask us to change who we are or become something we're not have failed us over and over again. Mindfulness recognizes and cultivates the best of who we are as human beings.

4. Mindfulness has the potential to become a transformative social phenomenon. Here's why:

5. Anyone can do it. Mindfulness practice cultivates universal human qualities and does not require anyone to change their beliefs. Everyone can benefit and it's easy to learn.

6. It's a way of living. Mindfulness is more than just a practice. It brings awareness and caring into everything we do—and it cuts down needless stress. Even a little makes our lives better.

7. It's evidence-based. We don't have to take mindfulness on faith. Both science and experience demonstrate its positive benefits for our health, happiness, work, and relationships.

8. It sparks innovation. As we deal with our world's increasing complexity and uncertainty, mindfulness can lead us to effective, resilient, low-cost responses to seemingly intransigent problems.

How Mindfulness Can Impact our Mental Health

Mindfulness can help us to improve our mental well-being in at least two ways. Mindfulness-based therapy and interventions take a more structured approach to addressing mental health symptoms, while less structured approaches can be found in many forms and cover a whole diversity of different topics. Let's look briefly at both.

Mindfulness-Based Therapies and Interventions

Given that anxiety and depression are two of the most prevalent mental illnesses in the world, it's unsurprising that two of the most well-known mindfulness-based interventions are focused on addressing these mental states.

Mindfulness-Based Stress Reduction (MBSR), pioneered by Dr. Kabat-Zinn at the UMass Stress Reduction School, is a group approach. It centers on the idea that a flexible range of mindfulness practices can be used to help people deal with the difficulties of stress and anxiety-related mental illness. Typically, this will involve a combination of yoga and/or mindfulness meditation, harnessing different techniques to relieve stress.

You can read more about MBSR at the Center for Mindfulness.

Mindfulness-Based Cognitive Therapy (MBCT) is also a group program, used to help those with recurring depression to reduce their symptoms and prevent relapse (Segal et al., 2002). MBCT involves both cognitive behavioral therapy (CBT) and mindfulness practices, such as mindful breathing and meditation. Acceptance is a central part of MBCT, in that participants learn approaches for re-framing, rather than eliminating their feelings.

Day-To-Day Mindfulness Practice

As you would expect, a lot of the more informal approaches to practicing mindfulness also feature meditation and yoga. It's also easy to sign up for classes, retreats, programs, and talks, but the easiest way to get started right away is to try special exercises that you can do at home. Head here for 25 MBSR exercises that you might like.

Can It Help Improve Our Wellbeing?

Yes! If the above benefits aren't enough to convince you, there are still more ways that practicing mindfulness can help improve your well-being.

Mindfulness can help you:

> Regulate and express your emotions

> Develop and utilize better coping strategies

> Be less easily distracted on non-task activities

> Help you sleep better

> Practice self-compassion

> Potentially, build resilience

Can Mindfulness Be Harmful?

Practicing mindfulness has some similarities to playing sports. Take a responsible approach to whatever

How Mindfulness Can Impact our Mental Health

Mindfulness can help us to improve our mental well-being in at least two ways. Mindfulness-based therapy and interventions take a more structured approach to addressing mental health symptoms, while less structured approaches can be found in many forms and cover a whole diversity of different topics. Let's look briefly at both.

Mindfulness-Based Therapies and Interventions

Given that anxiety and depression are two of the most prevalent mental illnesses in the world, it's unsurprising that two of the most well-known mindfulness-based interventions are focused on addressing these mental states.

Mindfulness-Based Stress Reduction (MBSR), pioneered by Dr. Kabat-Zinn at the UMass Stress Reduction School, is a group approach. It centers on the idea that a flexible range of mindfulness practices can be used to help people deal with the difficulties of stress and anxiety-related mental illness. Typically, this will involve a combination of yoga and/or mindfulness meditation, harnessing different techniques to relieve stress.

You can read more about MBSR at the Center for Mindfulness.

Mindfulness-Based Cognitive Therapy (MBCT) is also a group program, used to help those with recurring depression to reduce their symptoms and prevent relapse (Segal et al., 2002). MBCT involves both cognitive behavioral therapy (CBT) and mindfulness practices, such as mindful breathing and meditation. Acceptance is a central part of MBCT, in that participants learn approaches for re-framing, rather than eliminating their feelings.

Day-To-Day Mindfulness Practice

As you would expect, a lot of the more informal approaches to practicing mindfulness also feature meditation and yoga. It's also easy to sign up for classes, retreats, programs, and talks, but the easiest way to get started right away is to try special exercises that you can do at home. Head here for 25 MBSR exercises that you might like.

Can It Help Improve Our Wellbeing?

Yes! If the above benefits aren't enough to convince you, there are still more ways that practicing mindfulness can help improve your well-being.

Mindfulness can help you:

    Regulate and express your emotions

    Develop and utilize better coping strategies

    Be less easily distracted on non-task activities

    Help you sleep better

    Practice self-compassion

    Potentially, build resilience

Can Mindfulness Be Harmful?

Practicing mindfulness has some similarities to playing sports. Take a responsible approach to whatever practice you choose, and in most cases, you will generally be fine. Nonetheless, the massive rise in interest about mindfulness has prompted some research into its potential downsides. A few of these include

Forming false memories. Research by Wilson and colleagues (2015) provides results suggesting mindfulness meditation may make people more susceptible to fake memories. That is, participants who practiced mindfulness meditation in the study showed some impairments in their ability to monitor reality.

Mentally discarding positive thoughts as well as bad. Another study found that the mindfulness practice of 'discarding negative thoughts' may also lead us to discard positive and strengthening ones, too (Briñol et al., 2012). It's worth mentioning that this effect was much more noticeable when participants physically wrote down thoughts, then threw them away, rather than just imagining the scenario.

Avoid difficult thinking. Some practitioners may use mindfulness to avoid more cognitively taxing tasks, choosing to withdraw into a state of mindfulness rather than engage with a problem at hand

Physical and psychological symptoms. Some studies have found instances where mindfulness meditation has been linked to potential adverse reactions. These included derealization, depersonalization, and, amongst other things, hallucinations

If you're concerned about any of these findings, you might find the papers above to be interesting reading.

Mindfulness and other practices

Why Should We Practice Mindfulness?

There have been many prominent teachers like Deepak Chopra or Eckhart Tolle and others who teach us about the power of mindfulness and why it's so important to incorporate it into our daily practice. It has many proven benefits from reducing anxiety, depression and chronic pain to improving sleep and reducing stress. Mindfulness also helps us in achieving our goals such as weight-loss or starting a new project. And from a leadership perspective, mindfulness can help us stay centered in order to more effectively manage people or deal with external challenges. All in all, mindfulness is an important practice for us to cultivate to lead happy and meaningful lives.

But it's not something that comes naturally for us especially with the many distractions that take our attention and focus elsewhere. Most of us are now addicted to our technology and have less ability to focus our attention for a long period of time. We constantly check our news feed, email or texts and are bombarded with information overload. The day goes by without us even checking in with ourselves, let alone spending time practicing mindfulness, which ironically ends up making us feel disconnected and unhappy. And when we do slow down we tend to feel guilty for doing so, like there's some kind of rule that tells us we need to be busy in every given moment to be productive and make the most of each minute.

The result of this is we become much more susceptible to bad news, misinformation and anxiety which drag us down both mentally and physically. We end up being uncomfortable with just being with ourselves, we lose our connection to something bigger or to our inner power. We lose our ability to create our future consciously through focusing on what's working for us right now.

Since breaking our addiction to technology is a much bigger task (and a topic for another blog), we need to build practices in our daily lives to bring ourselves back to what really matters. Although nothing beats a good mindfulness meditation it can sometimes be difficult to squeeze in a 20-30 minute meditation in our busy lives. Instead, we can build micro-practices throughout the day to focus our attention.

What You Need to Know Before Practicing Mindfulness:

1. You don't need to buy anything. You can practice anywhere, there's no need to go out and buy a special cushion or bench—all you need is to devote a little time and space to accessing your mindfulness skills every day.

2. There's no way to quiet your mind. That's not the goal here. There's no bliss state or otherworldly communion. All you're trying to do is pay attention to the present moment, without judgment. Sounds easy, right?

3. Your mind will wander. As you practice paying attention to what's going on in your body and mind at the present moment, you'll find that many thoughts arise. Your mind might drift to something that happened yesterday, meander to your to-do list—your mind will try to be anywhere but where you are. But the wandering mind isn't something to fear, it's part of human nature and it provides the magic moment for the essential piece of mindfulness practice—the piece that researchers believe leads to healthier, more agile brains: the moment when you recognize that your mind has wandered. Because if you can notice that your mind has wandered, then you can consciously bring it back to the present moment. The more you do this, the more likely you are to be able to do it again and again. And that beats walking around on autopilot any day (ie: getting to your destination without remembering the drive, finding yourself with your hand in the bottom of a chip bag you only meant to snack a little from, etc.).

4. Your judgy brain will try to take over. The second part of the puzzle is the "without judgment" part. We're all guilty of listening to the critic in our heads a little more than we should. (That critic has saved us from disaster quite a few times.) But, when we practice investigating our judgments and diffusing them, we can learn to choose how we look at things and react to them. When you practice mindfulness, try not to judge yourself for whatever thoughts pop up. Notice judgments arise, make a mental note of them (some people label them "thinking"), and let them pass, recognizing the sensations they might leave in your body, and letting those pass as well.

5. It's all about returning your attention again and again to the present moment. It seems like our minds are wired to get carried away in thought. That's why mindfulness is the practice of returning, again and again, to the breath. We use the sensation of the breath as an anchor to the present moment. And every time we return to the breath, we reinforce our ability to do it again. Call it a bicep curl for your brain.

How to Practice Mindfulness

Each mindfulness class or session can be different, but here are a few things that you can expect. Mindfulness can be defined as paying attention, on purpose, to the present moment, without judgment. In order to create space of focus, mindfulness sessions typically take place in a space that is quiet and distraction free. Sessions often begin with a sitting practice, in which you will sit quietly, either on a chair or the floor, closing your eyes or allowing your gaze to rest softly on the space in front of you, focusing on either your breath or other body sensations. Many times, there is an opportunity to talk about your experience between practices. It is very normal for you r mind to be easily distracted during practice; the overall goal is to notice that distraction each time it happens and to bring your attention back to the area of focus. Being distracted is not a sign that you are doing it wrong! Instead, noticing that distraction is a sign that you are doing exactly what you should be. It can be useful to wear comfortable clothing, to facilitate sitting easily; you may want to wear shoes that are easy to slip off. None of that is required, though. It's also worth noting that if sitting is for any reason uncomfortable or difficult, mindfulness practices can be done standing up or lying down; some practices may involve moving, which can always be modified to meet your body's needs.

Mindful Practices for Every Day

As you spend time practicing mindfulness, you'll probably find yourself feeling kinder, calmer, and more patient. These shifts in your experience are likely to generate changes in other parts of your life as well.

Mindfulness can help you become more playful, maximize your enjoyment of a long conversation with a friend over a cup of tea, then wind down for a relaxing night's sleep. Try these 4 practices this week:u

1. Try This Simple Walking Meditation

Try these simple set of instructions for walking meditation, and keep this chart handy for practicing on-the-go.

TIME: 10 minutes

At some point today, you will most likely walk. You may even go for a walk.

It's one of our greatest gifts, and when we manage early in life to use our legs to get around, it's cause for celebration. Parents call their parents just to report on the event. The very fact that walking— or whatever form of ambulation you use to get around—is so central to our lives makes it a ready focus for mindful, meditative attention.

Here's a simple set of instructions for one form of walking meditation. There are many variations. This one relies on a pace that is close to how we might walk in everyday life, and in fact it can be adapted for walking in the street—just as long as you remember to pay attention to street lights, other people, and not looking like a zombie.

> Stand up STRAIGHT with your back upright but not stiff. Feel your feet touching the ground and let your weight distribute evenly.

> Curl the THUMB of your left hand in and wrap your fingers around it. Place it just above your belly button. Wrap your right hand around it, resting your

right thumb in the crevice formed between your left thumb and index finger. (This creates some balance for you and keeps your swinging arms from being a distraction.)

Drop your GAZE slightly. This helps you maintain focus.

Step out with your left FOOT. Feel it swing, feel the heel hit the ground, now the ball, now the toes.

FEEL the same as the right foot comes forward.

Walk at a STEADY pace, slightly slower than in daily life but not funereal. When your attention wanders, bring it back to the sensations of your feet touching the ground.

2. 5 Steps to Mindful Listening

Tips on how to be a good listener to yourself so you can be a better listener to others.

How often do you feel really listened to? How often do you really listen to others? (Be honest.)

We know we're in the presence of a good listener when we get that sweet, affirming feeling of really being heard. But sadly it occurs all too rarely. We can't force others to listen, but we can improve our own listening, and perhaps inspire others by doing so.

Good listening means mindful listening. Like mindfulness itself, listening takes a combination of intention and attention. The intention part is having a genuine interest in the other person—their experiences, views, feelings, and needs. The attention part is being able to stay present, open, and unbiased as we receive the other's words—even when they don't line up with our own ideas or desires.

Paradoxically, being good at listening to others requires the ability to listen to yourself. If you can't recognize your own beliefs and opinions, needs and fears, you won't have enough inner space to really hear anyone else. So the foundation for mindful listening is self-awareness.

Here are some tips to be a good listener to yourself so you can be a good listener for others.

How to Really Listen

Check inside: "How am I feeling just now? Is there anything getting in the way of being present for the other person?" If something is in the way, decide if it needs to be addressed first or can wait till later.

Feeling your own sense of presence, extend it to the other person with the intention to listen fully and openly, with interest, empathy, and mindfulness.

Silently note your own reactions as they arise—thoughts, feelings, judgments, memories. Then return your full attention to the speaker.

Reflect back what you are hearing, using the speaker's own words when possible, paraphrasing or summarizing the main point. Help the other person feel heard.

Use friendly, open-ended questions to clarify your understanding and probe for more. Affirm before you differ. Acknowledge the other person's point of view—acknowledging is not agreeing!—before introducing your own ideas, feelings, or requests.

People often find some difficulty in caring for themselves, in receiving love, in believing they deserve to be happy.

Imagine for a moment the amount of energy you expend brooding over the future, ruminating about the past, comparing yourself to others, judging yourself, worrying about what might happen next. That is a huge amount of energy. Now imagine all of that energy gathered in and returned to you. Underlying our usual patterns of self-preoccupation, stinging self-judgment, and fear is the universal, innate potential for love and awareness.

Loving-kindness meditations point us back to a place within, where we can cultivate love and help it flourish. Developing care toward ourselves is the first objective, the foundation for later being able to include others in the sphere of kindness.

How to Do a Loving-Kindness Meditation

This loving-kindness practice involves silently repeating phrases that offer good qualities to oneself and to others.

You can start by taking delight in your own goodness—calling to mind things you have done out of good-heartedness, and rejoicing in those memories to celebrate the potential for goodness we all share.

Silently recite phrases that reflect what we wish most deeply for ourselves in an enduring way. Traditional phrases are:
• May I live in safety.

• May I have mental happiness (peace, joy).
• May I have physical happiness (health, freedom from pain).
• May I live with ease.

Repeat the phrases with enough space and silence between so they fall into a rhythm that is pleasing to you. Direct your attention to one phrase at a time

Each time you notice your attention has wandered, be kind to yourself and let go of the distraction. Come back to repeating the phrases without judging or disparaging yourself.

After some time, visualize yourself in the center of a circle composed of those who have been kind to you, or have inspired you because of their love. Perhaps you've met them, or read about them; perhaps they live now, or have existed historically or even mythically. That is the circle. As you visualize yourself in the center of it, experience yourself as the recipient of their love and attention. Keep gently repeating the phrases of loving kindness for yourself.

To close the session, let go of the visualization, and simply keep repeating the phrases for a few more minutes. Each time you do so, you are transforming your old, hurtful relationship to yourself, and are moving forward, sustained by the force of kindness.

4. 5 Steps to Wind Down and Fall Asleep

A bedtime meditation to stop tossing and turning, and get some quality shut-eye.

As someone who works every day with patients struggling with insomnia, the most common thing I hear is once the head hits the pillow, the brain doesn't stop. They know sleep should come, but the brain just wants to think about both pressing and mundane things, such as reviewing the day's events and tasks that need to be completed.

When we lose awareness of the present moment, our minds get stuck in maladaptive ways of thinking. For example, you might be trying to go to sleep but your mind gets lost thinking about all the groceries you need to buy. Deep, relaxed breathing is forgotten. And once you realize sleep isn't happening, your muscles tense and your thought process quickly shifts to "I'm not falling asleep! I have XYZ to do this week and I won't be able to function tomorrow." The body seizes up, breathing and heart rate can both quicken, and falling sleep becomes more difficult.

> When we lose awareness of the present moment, our minds get stuck in maladaptive ways of thinking.

Newer models of insomnia treatment are beginning to incorporate mindfulness. Here's a grounding exercise to help you get some quality shut-eye.

A Five-Step Sleep Meditation

Dim the lights 1 hour before bedtime. Start winding down the brain and body by dimming the lights. Engage in relaxing activities outside the bedroom that pass the time quietly.

Avoid looking at anything with a screen. Stow away your tablet, phone, computer, and TV for the night—the light can keep you awake and alert.

Ten minutes before bedtime, begin a focused mindfulness exercise. Sit in a comfortable chair in the same dimly lit room. Imagine the outline of your body and slowly trace it in your head. Keep in mind the amount of pressure you're feeling against the chair or the ground and be mindful of where there's more pressure and where there's less. Start with your head. Is it touching the back of the chair? How heavy does it feel against the chair, wall, or just the air? Then slowly move down to your ear, then shoulder, arm, and leg. Work down to your feet and then back up the other side of your body. Take about five minutes for this exercise.

If your mind begins to wander, notice that it wandered and get back on track. Try to avoid judging yourself—your mind will indeed wander; the skill lies in getting it back on track.

If your mind begins to wander, notice that it wandered and get back on track. Try to avoid judging yourself—your mind will indeed wander; the skill lies in getting it back on track.

Want to try mindfulness on your own?

Maybe you can't make it to a mindfulness group session during the week, or maybe you want to expand your practice to create some consistency for yourself. You can incorporate mindfulness into your everyday routine in many ways – research has shown that regular practice, even short 5-10 minute practices, can be even more effective than one or two long practices each week. The point here is to do what you can and not to judge yourself!

Here is a list of some types of mindfulness practices that you can incorporate into your own daily practice (you may encounter some of these in classes, as well):

Breath meditation: To begin meditating, find a comfortable and quiet place. Sit on a cushion or chair, with an erect yet relaxed posture. Close your eyes gently and begin by bringing your full and present attention to whatever you feel within and around you. You may want to take a number of deep, cleansing breaths to center and calm yourself before letting your breath return to normal. Allow yourself to become more and more still. Do your best to remain focused on the experience of your breath, knowing that it is natural for thoughts to arise and distract you. As soon as you are aware that you have become distracted, observe that you have become distracted and return your attention, with kindness, to the breath. There's no failure or shame in distraction; we are slowly training our minds to be focused and present. If you are new to meditation, start small.

> A short guided breath meditation (3 minutes) can be found here:
> 3-minute Mindful Breathing Meditation (Relieve Stress)

> A slightly longer one (9 minutes) 9 Minute Breathing Meditation mp4

> A visualization practice with breath and chakra opening (17 minutes)

Mindful eating: The goal of mindful eating is to bring your full and complete attention to the food that you are eating, and to the experience of eating that food. Take time to first look at the food, appreciating the colors and textures, the contrasts between the food and the plate it is on. Think about where the food came from – who was involved in getting that food to your plate? Savor the smells of the food before ever taking a bite, and notice how your body responds – does your mouth water? Are you anticipating that first bite? Take each bite slowly, noticing the changing tastes and smells, and paying attention to your body as you eat your meal. Notice when you begin to feel full; notice if you are thirsty. Even giving this kind of ttention to the first three or four bites of a meal is a good regular practice.

Mindfulness of other daily practices: You can bring a similar type of mindful curiosity to other everyday practices, such as brushing your teeth, taking a shower, walking the dog, or doing the dishes. One way to incorporate mindfulness into your day might be to choose one of those activities and to engage with it as mindfully as possible each day, attending to each changing sensation that arises and falls away as you do that activity.

Body scan: Another practice that you may experience in a mindfulness class or session is the body scan. This is also a practice you can do at home. Find a comfortable place to lie down or to sit, if lying is uncomfortable, or you feel that you are likely to fall asleep. Moving your awareness slowly from either your feet to your head or vice versa, pay curious and close attention to the sensations you feel in each part of your body; if you feel nothing, that's OK. There are many excellent guided body scans available online, if that helps you to know how and when to move from body part to body part.

Walking Meditation: Sometimes it is hard to sit still and meditate. Walking meditation is a very common type of moving meditation during which you focus your attention on the experience of walking. In this practice, try to bring your awareness to each aspect of walking – lifting your foot, moving the foot forward, placing the foot on the ground, and shifting your weight onto the stepping foot. As you walk slowly and naturally, tune into sensations that you might normally take for granted, such as your breath moving through your body, the sensations of moving your feet and legs, or the ways your arms or hips move as you walk.

Lovingkindness Meditation: Lovingkindness meditation is generally a guided meditation which uses words or images to call forth feelings of kindness and compassion for ourselves and others. This practice is usually preceded by at least a short period of silent meditation of your choice to ground and calm yourself. Lovingkindness meditations use varying words and images, so find a version which feels right to you.

How Do I Bring More Mindfulness Into My Life?

How To Begin Practicing Mindfulness

At its core, mindfulness is an activity that needs to be practiced, exercised, and adopted. With these cornerstones in mind – practice, exercise, adopt – let's consider a few ways to introduce mindfulness into our daily lives.

Start with a daily routine

The first step is to introduce a daily routine. Like any exercise, mindfulness benefits from regular practice. In research where mindfulness is used as an intervention, researchers often use an intervention plan that takes place across many weeks

Decide on an uninterrupted time of day that you can set aside to practice mindfulness, and keep that time in your schedule.

Mindfulness is a way of perceiving, thinking, and behaving

You would be forgiven for thinking that mindfulness is just an activity; in fact, mindfulness is a way of perceiving and observing, and it can be developed using various tools. Some of these tools include meditation, exercises, and breathing.

Commit, commit, commit

The most important step before embarking on this journey is to commit to it. Some meta-analyses have highlighted that some studies found varying effects for mindfulness interventions, and the authors posit that this might be because the participants are not engaging in their mindfulness homework or exercises, or do these exercises for too short a period to see results

Therefore, knowing this, before you begin, you have to commit. Now, if you're ready, I'm going to convince you why you should start a mindfulness routine, and I'll explain how to live a mindful life daily.

5 Reasons to Start Practicing Mindfulness Today

At this point, you might think that mindfulness sounds like it requires a lot of effort.

Beginning a mindfulness habit is work, and it will be difficult in the beginning, but this habit will become easier over time and with more practice.

Additionally, mindfulness has numerous positive benefits, which is supported by research. Some of the benefits of mindfulness include emotional benefits, cognitive benefits, interpersonal benefits, professional benefits, and practical benefits.

Emotional benefits

Regular mindfulness meditation results in reduced depressive symptoms, negative affect, and rumination. Rumination is the persistent over-worry of

- past events,

- negative emotions, and

- both the cause and consequences of these emotions

Rumination is often linked to increased depression and anxiety. Read our related article on Mindful Thinking, where we discuss four ways to stop ruminating.

The positive effects of mindfulness at reducing negative affect and other negative psychological syndromes, like depression and anxiety, are not limited to only one study. Instead, these findings are supported in a meta-analysis by Hoffman et al.

In that meta-analysis, which contained 39 studies, the effect sizes for the differences in the psychological state before and after the mindful therapy was large for clinical participants and moderate for nonclinical participants.

These results suggest that therapeutic interventions based on mindfulness are not only successful for clinical populations, but the benefits extend to nonclinical populations.

Cognitive benefits

Practitioners of mindfulness have better working memory than nonpractitioners which allows for better emotional regulation.

Participants also report that their attention improves significantly after regular mindful meditation compared to before they began mindful meditation

There is also some laboratory evidence that suggests that people who have developed a habit of practicing mindfulness for longer are better at ignoring emotional distractions than people whose mindfulness habit is shorter or who do not practice mindfulness

These results suggest that the benefits of mindfulness are cumulative and will continue to improve over time.

Interpersonal benefits

The benefits of mindfulness flow to other spheres of life, including relationships.

There is some evidence that regular mindfulness practice can improve relationship satisfaction and communication through a variety of paths specifically:

- Responding to relationship stress in a positive way

- Better identification of one's own emotions

- Better communication of one's own emotions

- Better conflict resolution

- Improved empathy

Professional benefits

It should come as no surprise that the benefits of mindfulness are not limited to interpersonal relationships only – for example, the ability to communicate clearly and to respond more effectively to stressful situations should translate from personal to professional contexts

Empirical evidence also exists that shows that employees who practice regularly mindful activities experienced higher job satisfaction and lower job stress than a control group who did not participate

6 Simple Tips to Practice Mindfulness Every Day

1. Allow your mind to wander. Especially if you practice for even a few breaths or for a few minutes. Practice kindness and patience with yourself when this happens and gently return awareness to the breath sensation.

2. Notice any tendency to be hard on yourself or to feel frustrated or a failure. See this kind of judgment as just another kind of thinking, and gently return awareness to the breath.

3. Embrace relaxation, especially if you practice for even a few breaths or for a few moments. This relaxed feeling is an ally. It helps us to be more present, more mindful. Relaxation alone is not what mindfulness is about, however! It is about being present with awareness.

4. Expect to notice more things, including more painful things. This is actually progress. You are not doing anything wrong! Quite the opposite, you are increasing mindfulness for all things. When you begin to notice the painful things, see if you can hold yourself with compassion and kindness, and continue to bring open-hearted awareness to the experience that is unfolding.

5. Practice staying present. By not turning away from the painful things in our lives, we can learn to remain open to all the possibilities in each situation. This increases our chances for healing and transformation in meeting the pain we face. And it also gives us a way to be with those situations when there is nothing more we can do to "get away from the pain" but must find a way to be with it. We can discover that the quality of mindfulness is not destroyed or damaged by contact with pain, that it can know pain as completely and fully as it knows any other experience.

6. Be careful not to try too hard. Don't try to make anything happen, or to achieve any special states or any special effects! Simply relax and pay as much attention as you can to just what is here now. Whatever form that takes. Allow yourself to experience life directly as it unfolds, paying careful and open-hearted attention.

How Mindfulness Helps Us Be More Present

Our reactions to the stressful events of our lives can become so habituated that they occur essentially out of our awareness, until, because of physical or emotional or psychological dysfunction, we cannot ignore them any longer. These reactions can include tensing the body, experiencing painful emotional states, even panic and depression, and being prisoners of habits of thinking and self-talk including obsessional list making, and intense, even toxic self-criticism.

> All we have to do is to establish attention in the present moment, and to allow ourselves to be with what is here.

So, we can practice mindfulness and become more present. All we have to do is to establish attention in the present moment, and to allow ourselves to be with what is here. To rest in the awareness of what is here. To pay attention without trying to change anything. To allow ourselves to become more deeply and completely aware of what it is we are sensing. And to be with what it is we are experiencing. To rest in this quality of being, of being aware, in each moment as our life unfolds.

And, to the extent we can practice "being" and become more present and more aware of our life and in our life, the "doing" we do about all of it, will be more informed, more responsive, and less driven by the habits of reaction and inattention.

Make the effort! Whenever you think of it in your day or night, remember that you can be more mindful. See for yourself what it might be like to pay more careful attention and to allow yourself to experience directly

21 simple mindfulness exercises to improve your focus

When you are distracted, unaware of what you are doing, the end product suffers. Mindfulness is not just a state of mind—your (lack of) focus affects your craft.

If greater well-being isn't enough motivation for you, scientists have discovered that mindfulness techniques improve self-control, objectivity, tolerance, enhanced flexibility, concentration, and empathy—you gain mental clarity.

You probably know all this. But, also fear that I will tell you that meditation is the way to go. I get a lot of people asking me for other ways to become more mindful. Many have already tried meditation before and, after a few frustrating attempts, they quit. Others think meditation is not for them. If that's your case, no worries. This post has you covered.

I'm not writing off meditation, neither telling you to do so. But, there are many other ways to start practicing everyday mindfulness.

A quick note on the difference between mindfulness and meditation. Though these two words seem interchangeable, they are not the same.

Mindfulness is the quality of being present—the experience of being open and aware in the moment, without judgment or criticism, focusing your mind on the present rather than wandering. Meditation is the practice of training your mind for everyday mindfulness. You learn to strengthen your mind as you become more familiar with yourself.

List of Mindfulness Exercises

1. Watch your own movie

Imagine you are observing a movie and have to describe everything that is happening to someone else. You have to pay special attention and be clear, so the other person can understand what's going on.

That's precisely the purpose of this exercise. The only thing is that the movie is your life and you are telling the story to yourself, not to someone else. When you are ready, start by focusing on what you are doing—describe everything that is going on. Be specific, detailed-oriented, and clear. You are trying to increase awareness of how you are doing what you are doing.

Most of the time, we are living on autopilot. This exercise will help you increase awareness of your behavior, no matter how insignificant or not is the task that you are performing.

2. Observe other people

We usually see reality, but we don't honestly pay attention. Similar to the previous exercise, you will increase your focus by becoming a better observer. You can practice this at your office or in a public space such as a park or public transportation.

Focus on one person and observe what that s/he is doing. Look at the appearance, body language, the way s/he is dressed. Then, move to another person or group and repeat the observation. You are not trying to guess or interpret what they are doing or why. Just watch and become aware of what's going on.

We usually don't pay attention to what happens right in front of our eyes. And, if we do, we pass judgment. When we judge people by their looks or actions, we stop seeing. Becoming more mindful requires to see things as they are, not through the lens of our feelings.

3. Slow down

When you rush from one thing to another, you are doing stuff but not performing at your best. By slowing down, you can reconnect with the present moment and flow.

Taking more time to do something will help you appreciate what you are doing as well as improve your end product. Most of our mistakes are made not out of ignorance but of being sloppy. As the saying goes, there is never enough time to do it right the first time, but always enough time to do it over.

Slowing down doesn't mean being slow. When we find balance, we become more productive and effective—we don't need to do things over.

When you enjoy what you are doing, there's no need to rush from one task to another. Instead of just checking things off your list, you learn to enjoy the journey too

4. 5-minute breathing exercise

This exercise is short and easy. Don't tell me you can't make five minutes for yourself. Breathing is a necessary process to stay alive. Sounds obvious, right? However, when we are anxious, what do we do? We stop breathing, or we don't breathe as regularly and deep as we should.

Yogis count life not in years but in the number of breaths they take. Certain apps, such as Spire, were designed for that purpose: to help you track your breathing. However, the best way to improve your breathing is to practice paying attention—you don't need an app for that.

Find a comfortable position. You can either be seated on a chair or the floor. Keep your back upright (but don't force it). Notice your body and relax. Take a deep breath and focus on the experience.

Feel the natural rhythm of your breath. Notice the air temperature in and out. Let your breath flow naturally. You don't need to do anything. Your body knows how to breathe on its own—don't force it. Notice how your chest expands and contracts. Focus on your body—one breath at a time.

You might get distracted at some point. That's okay. Don't judge yourself. You can say "thinking" and let your thoughts flow naturally. Reconnect with your breath. When the five minutes are up, focus on your breath one more time. You are all set.

Practicing this exercise daily, will improve your breathing but also bring calmness and more awareness to your life. When we increase self-awareness, we become at peace with ourselves.

5. The body scan

This is a popular exercise among mindfulness practitioners. And a favorite among beginners.

Mindfulness requires to pay attention to both our mind and body. Pain is a signal—where do you feel it and why? Your body registers everything that happens to you. When we have muscle knots is because our mind is full of tensions too.

Practice this exercise more than once a day. When you are brushing your teeth, waiting for the bus or in an elevator—every spare moment is an excellent opportunity to practice a body scan. Overcome the instinct to grab your phone—like we all do when we are in between things—and focus on your body.

Take a deep breath. Scan your head, face, neck,

shoulders, chest, legs, and arms. Focus your breath on the area where you feel pain—the oxygen provides calmness and relaxation. This video will help you improve your practice.

6. Observe with your eyes closed

Our eyes are our primary source of distraction—we jump from one thing to another and stop paying attention. Sometimes, the best way to remove a distraction is to stop seeing it.

This is ideal to practice in a public space. Close your eyes. Take a deep breath and relax. Focus on what's going on around you. First, pay attention to the sounds that are closer to you. Little by little, start focusing on the sounds that are farther away.

Now, pay attention to what's going on right next to you. What sounds do you hear? Can you hear voices? What are they saying?

Now repeat the same routine with the more distant noises, sounds, and voices. Remember that you are trying to understand, not to analyze, what's happening.

Pay attention—learn to observe what's going on without seeing.

7. The tangerine experience

This exercise is about improving our ability to focus on the details. You can practice this with a tomato, walnut or any other fruit of your choice too. I love tangerines because they have a unique shape and texture.

Take a look at the fruit. Pay attention to its shape. Touch it and notice how it feels. Play with it. See how the shape and texture react to your manipulation. Smell the fruit. Now close your eyes and smell it again.

Hold your breath for a second or two and see how long the perfume stays.

By focusing on one fruit, you practice paying attention. Everything else fades away when you concentrate on one single thing. Mindfulness is about noticing what's happening right in front of you in the present moment.

8. Track footsteps

We are so busy looking that we stop seeing. Tracking is the art of interpreting the indirect signs left by animals or people. It's an entertaining and insightful practice once you get used to it.

The purpose of this exercise is to notice the tracks but also trying to understand what left them behind.

The other day, my wife and I were walking in the middle of a park in Wisconsin right after a massive ice storm. All of a sudden, I noticed some deer tracks. I stopped to observe them in more detail. I realized there were two pairs—one smaller, one bigger. Probably, a mom with the calf. I followed their path and saw how they run in one direction and then turned back in the opposite way. The tracks seemed fresh—the shape was still perfect. As I continue to observe, I noticed that some tracks were deeper than others, with a more significant distance in between—maybe both the deer were running or jumping at that point.

I'm not a track expert by any means. But observing footprints is an excellent way to train our focus. What seems like a silly exercise at first, makes us feel calm and curious about our surroundings.

Snow and sand are perfect for tracking footsteps, but you can also practice in a park or any other public space.

9. Turn your chores into a meditation

Mindfulness is more than just noticing things—you learn to enjoy what you are doing. We all hate chores. However, the more we avoid doing something, the more burdensome that task becomes.

Choose a chore that you want to master or one that you usually do but dislike. Prepare by setting-up the scenario—remove distractions or things that might get in the way.

Focus on the activity. Let's say you want to clean the kitchen. Start by visualizing the outcome. How would you like the kitchen to look like? How will you feel once you've accomplished the task?

Start doing the chore. Pay attention to every detail. Observe your movements. How can you improve your craft? Experiment with alternative ways. Which one works better? How do you feel when you improvise instead of repeating the same movement over and over?

Keep the end-result present. You are not just do-ing something. You want to become the best kitchen cleaner ever. Once you are finished, take some time to appreciate the outcome. You can practice this with the same chore next time or with a different one.

10. The mindful window

Distance drives perspective—we get to see what was around us but were missing. Find a window. Look at everything you see. Start by the things that are closer to you and then, progressively, move your focus to those that are farther away.

Avoid judging or labeling things. Forget about the object—don't name things. Focus on the shapes, colors, movements, or textures. Don't pay attention to the sounds either. This exercise is about increasing focus by developing your ability to see things.

This practice requires just a few minutes yet increases our ability to discover new things even in familiar places. The more you train your ability to observe, the more things you'll see.

11. Mindful listening

This exercise is for a group setting and requires a moderator. Pair up all participants.

Each person shares a personal story or anecdote with her/his partner. Everyone has the same time: 3 minutes. Then they switch roles. Once everyone is done, the moderator asks participants to share with their partner the story they told them—try to be as accurate as possible and to use the same words the other person used. Switch roles again.

Now, participants have to tell the story they heard but in the first person—like if it was their story. Then their partners do the same. Everyone comments on the experience: how accurate their partners were, and how they felt to tell someone else's story as if it was theirs.

The purpose of this exercise is to realize our ability to pay attention. But, most importantly, the effect that mind-wandering can have on others. While listening to their story being retold by others, most people realize we are not good listeners— a gentle reminder for everyday conversations.

12. Name your emotions

We are continually experiencing emotions. Sometimes, we don't pay attention to what we feel. Others, we overreact without realizing what's triggering our behavior.

This exercise will help you familiarize with your feelings. Practice labeling your emotions as they happen. Close your eyes and focus on your emotions. Name them without passing judgment. Feeling upset is not the same as being angry, sad, or frustrated. Most of the times, we mix our emotions. Check this post to learn to discriminate different feelings.

Becoming more mindful about how you feel can help you uncover what affects your mood but, most importantly, to avoid overreacting because you are not fully aware of what you are feeling.

The more you get to know your feelings, the less they will cloud your behavior.

13. Mindful gratitude

One of our principal sources of frustration is that we are living in the future—we anticipate what's going to happen instead of appreciating the here and now.

When we are consumed with our thoughts, worries, or dramas, we stop paying attention. Feeling grateful requires noticing everything that happens in our life. We are wired to focus on negative things—the ones that didn't happen as expected or went wrong. Practicing daily gratitude boots our happiness by grounding us to the present.

Reserve some time, preferably before you go to sleep, to capture all the good stuff that you should be thankful for. Recap your day, and think of all the people you met, all the moments you enjoyed, what you achieved or learned, the small battles you won.

Keeping a gratitude journal is an excellent practice, as I explain how to do it here. Our brain tends to focus on adverse events—this exercise could be a little bit frustrating until you get used to it. With time and practice, it'll become easier and easier to acknowledge all the positive stuff in your life.

14. Mindful eating

Food is much more than fuel to your body. It's a sensorial experience that can be both gratifying and insightful. Most eating disorders are anything but mindful—instead of enjoying eating we turn it into compulsive behavior.

Mindful eating is not just about appreciating the food but also understanding why you are eating.

Fortunately, most of us don't suffer from hunger. The downside is that our bodies don't know what that feeling really is. We eat because we are conditioned—driven by emotions, not a physical need. We feel a compulsion to eat. When other people are eating around us, we feel the urge to eat too. Or we have breakfast or lunch because it's the appropriate time, not because we are hungry.

Mindful eating is about becoming more aware of our relationship with food. Start by enjoying the smell and visual appearance of what you are going to eat. Don't just swallow the food, taste it. Cut small bites. Chew your food mindfully—it will help you eat less compulsively. Chewing may help you feel fuller longer, leading to less eating overall.

Snacking is a clear example of compulsory eating. Before you grab something in-between meals, ask yourself: "Am I really hungry? Why do I want to eat this now?"

When you feel the desire to eat, reflect on your feelings first. Most of the time, we eat to silence our emotions. If you are feeling distracted, anxious or upset, rather than eating try going out for a walk or engaging in another mindful task.

15. Mindful drinking

We tend to drink the way we do everything: fast. Not only we end drinking more than we planned, but we don't really enjoy what we are having. There's a growing movement in England promoting total cleansing. Non-alcoholic beverages—beer, spirits, wine, etc.—are on the rise and have decreased alcohol consumption among young people.

However, if you enjoy drinking and don't have a drinking problem, you can still do it mindfully. Just like with food, don't let your emotions control your behavior. Drink because you enjoy it, not to get rid of your problems. Drink because you want to, not because of social pressure. Drink to enjoy it, not to get drunk.

The problem with alcohol is that we are not taught to appreciate what we drink—we just swallow it.

Start by appreciating the moment. Enjoy the holistic experience. First, feel the glass. Notice its temperature and texture. Focus on the color. What do you see? What do you notice?

Swirl the wine (or drink) slowly. Observe the legs that it leaves behind in the glass. Take a slow deep breath in to inhale all of the aromas. What do the smells remind you of? Take a slow sip. Allow all of the different flavors to swish around your palette. Experience the wine, don't just drink it.

Concentrate on how it feels, tastes, and the memories or sensations it evokes. You can practice this exercise with coffee, tea, or even water too.

16. Declutter your workspace

Marie Kondo is very in right now. But you don't have to go to that extreme to clear your mind.

A cluttered desk is a cluttered mind. But there's more about cleaning your workspace. When you approach your work with mindfulness, you enjoy it more. Turn the act of clearing and organizing your desk into a mindful moment. Don't think of it as a chore but rather as setting up the right conditions to perform at your best.

My desk usually looks chaotic. I'm working on various client projects, researching, writing, preparing workshops or talks, etc. I feel the need to have my notes, post-its, and books in front of me. My desktop is also full of various open windows and files. I perform well in my organized chaos but, at some point, it starts to slow me down. So, I take a break to organize my stuff.

The act of decluttering not only helps me recover focus but also reenergizes me—it's like a gift to myself. Some people like it tidy; some thrive in chaos. Whatever your style is, decluttering your desk cleanses your mind.

17. Pay attention to music

We all love to enjoy music. Listening to music not only calms us, but it can also change our brain improving memory and learning. However, most of the times, we are not actively listening to the music—the sound becomes part of the background.

Practice paying attention to music. Choose any song and listen to it mindfully. Notice the different i nstruments. Try to identify each one of them. Now choose one—either the bass or drums—and just pay attention to it. If you really focus, at some point you will stop listening to the other instruments. Switch to the guitar or piano and repeat the exercise. Now listen to the entire song all over again. Pay attention to all instruments playing together. You will enjoy a much richer experience.

Practice paying attention to music. Choose any song and listen to it mindfully. Notice the different instruments. Try to identify each one of them. Now choose one—either the bass or drums—and just pay attention to it. If you really focus, at some point you will stop listening to the other instruments. Switch to the guitar or piano and repeat the exercise. Now listen to the entire song all over again. Pay attention to all instruments playing together. You will enjoy a much richer experience.

The power of this exercise goes beyond listening mindfully—paying attention helps us notice all the parts within the whole.

18. Silent meeting

We have a love-hate relationship with meetings. Most executives spend 25–30% of their working hours in a conference. The problem is not the time spent, but the quality—we usually don't pay attention to what other people are doing or saying.

Next time, try to stay silent. Focus on listening rather than on speaking up. Pay particular attention to other participants' behavior. Take notes—capture verbatims, not just the idea. Register the 'how,' not just what people are saying. Each person has a distinct way of expressing her/himself. We usually filter other people's words through our emotions or our ideas.

What happens when you really pay attention?

It's okay for you to speak up when necessary. But fight

the urge to do so. Are you going to say something new or just repeat what someone else said? Are you adding to the conversation? Will your words build on other people's ideas or deviate the focus?

This exercise will help you become a better listener, but also to be more mindful about what you say and when to speak up or not.

19. Body stretch

Working at a desk all day is harmful—we tend to adopt postures that make us feel stiff and tense. Regular stretching increases your flexibility—an essential factor of fitness—as well as improves your posture, reduces stress and body aches.

Inadequate flexibility not only harms your body but can accelerate reduced mobility that comes with age. Also, there's a direct correlation between our physical flexibility and our mental one. When you stretch your body, you are flexing your mind too.

Static stretches involve holding a stretch in a comfortable position for some time—between 10 to 30 seconds. It's beneficial after exercising. Dynamic stretches are active movements without holding the stretch. It's usually practiced before exercise. Try these 12 simple stretching exercises at your desk.

If you want to dive deeper, The book Stretching by Bob Anderson is a classic—it provides different routines and exercises for multiple age, activities, and sports.

Like everything, go slow. Be gentle with your muscles, or you can harm them. Your body needs time to adjust and get used to being stretched.

20. Take a digital break

When we feel overwhelmed, our first instinct is to find

comfort in our devices—we want to connect to something. However, this meaningless fix makes us feel more stressed out and distracted. Mind-wandering is driven by the lack of a connection with the present moment. Instead of focusing on one thing, our attention is divided.

Trying to reconnect to something is important, but it has to be something meaningful. Try taking a couple of digital breaks along the day. Start small—a 5-minute one is a good way to start. Little by little, increase the duration. When you achieve longer breaks (30 minutes or even one hour), you'll realize what a difference it makes.

Stepping away from your digital devices relaxes your mind. When we pause, we make room for new ideas to show up. Mental breaks boost our productivity, energy, and focus.

One word of caution. Many people fail to take a digital break because they approach it with the wrong mind-set. This is not about "devices are evil; get rid of them." It's rather about enjoying a mindful pause—to give your mind some space and calmness.

21. Walking contemplation

Most people associate meditation with being seated and relaxed. But you can also meditate while moving around. A walking contemplation is a simple way to practice a "meditation on-the-go."

Walking is a healthy habit—it increases your heart and lung fitness, improves balance and reduces body fat. When you can engage all your senses, it also calms your mind. That's the primary purpose of a walking contemplation—you are not just exercising your body but your mind too.

Ideally, plan for a 30-minute walk—that's the daily minimum recommended by health experts.

A walking contemplation is an invitation to engage all your senses. You become aware of how your body moves, feeling your feet hitting the ground, noticing what happens around you, listening to the sounds of people and objects, and noticing the air temperature as you breathe in and out.

When you engage with your environment, you paying attention to the present moment. You focus your energy on noticing things outside rather than ruminating thoughts inside your head.

Common Mindfulness Questions

1. Is there a wrong way to meditate? A right way to meditate?

People think they're messing up when they're meditating because of how busy the mind is. But getting lost in thought, noticing it, and returning to your chosen meditation object— breath, sound, body sensation, or something else—is how it's done. That's about it. If you're doing that, you're doing it right!

2. Are there more formal ways to take up mindfulness practice?

Mindfulness can be practiced solo, anytime, or with like-minded friends. But there are others ways, and many resources, to tap into. Mindfulness-Based Stress Reduction, Mindfulness-Based Cognitive Therapy, and other mindfulness-based trainings are available across North America. We've organized a list of centers here.

Daily guided meditations are also available by smartphone app, or you can practice in person at a meditation center. Read more about the types of programs currently available.

3. Do I have to practice every day?

No, but being that it's a beneficial practice, you may well find that the more you do it, the more you'll find it beneficial to your life. Read Jack Kornfield's guidelines for developing a daily practice here.

4. How do I find a meditation instructor?

If you want to make mindfulness a part of your life, you'll probably want to consider working with a meditation teacher or instructor. You can even do that online using a video chat format of some kind, but even then the same principles apply. Here are 4 questions to consider when looking for a meditation teacher:

1) Do you have good chemistry with them?

2) Are they open and accessible?

3) Do they have a deep understanding of the practice?

4) Could they regard you like a friend?

5. How do yoga and mindfulness work together?

There are a number of yoga poses that will help you with your mindfulness meditation practice. Here are 10 simple yoga exercises to reduce stress, improve well-being, and get you primed for a sitting meditation session—or anytime.

www.ingramcontent.com/pod-product-compliance
Lightning Source LLC
Chambersburg PA
CBHW021355160726
47994CB00007B/2960